In Appreciation of Life and All of its Little Things

Bettina Rosch

BookLeaf
Publishing

India | USA | UK

Presentation by *BookLeaf Publishing*

Web: www.bookleafpub.com

E-mail: info@bookleafpub.com

ISBN : 9789357611824

First edition 2021

DEDICATION

This is dedicated to all of the people who have never stopped believing in me and who inspired me to see things in myself that I never realised were there. This is also dedicated to the people who keep on waking up every day and getting themselves out of bed regardless of how they're feeling. This is your reminder to say you're doing great and to just keep taking things one day at a time.

ACKNOWLEDGEMENT

I would like to express my sincere thanks to my parents, Raymond and Grace, and my sister, Kira, for constantly supporting me in all of my endeavours; from listening to drafts to sharing my excitement over the opportunity.

This project would not have been possible without my best friends Joshua and Alystra Redmayne. You both constantly empower me to achieve so many things I had never thought were possible. Your encouragement and support has helped me to surpass my own personal expectations time and time again and I look forward to continuing to return the favour for you both in the many years to come.

I would also like to thank my good friend Zoe for introducing me to the opportunity to write this book and for giving me the extra push that I needed to commit to it. Here's to many more years of helping one another push those personal boundaries further and further.

PREFACE

Wanting to be a constantly positive person and influence for my students, and the people around me, means that I often need to pick myself up and be the first person to look on the brighter side of things in order to lead by genuine example. It's all too easy to focus on the negativity all around, particularly in the midst of a pandemic, but sometimes all it takes is a helping hand or a gentle nudge to start seeing past all of that. By allowing yourself to take a step back and reevaluate the things you thought you already knew, you open yourself up to a whole new way of viewing the rest of the world.

In appreciation of Hello

Ciao! Konnichiwa! Hola! And Hello!
Thank you so much for coming, I hope you
enjoy the show.
It might not be life-changing but I hope to give
some insight,
To all the things we might take for granted every
day and night.

Not everything will resonate or strike you to
your core,
But I'm hoping that nothing in here will strike
you as a bore.
Hello, my name is Bettina and I'm nothing if not
insecure,
But as bleak as life can seem sometimes, I know
it's so much more.

It's the little things, you see, that make life such
a treat,
From the notes that refuse to leave our heads, to
all the wonderful things we eat!
Let's embark on this journey together, exploring
all things great and small,
Starting with the very word which can initiate a
call.

Hello? Hello, my friend! Hallo! Wie geht's es
dir?
If I move outside, is my voice right now a little
bit more clear?
Sometimes the word comes out on purpose,
sometimes involuntarily,
For a friend you haven't seen in years or if
something brushes past your knee.

It's the word that's by your side when you think
you're all alone,
Yet suddenly you hear a bump... when no one
else is home...
Is it a cat? Was it a rat?! Surely not something
beneath your hat.
A sigh of relief as you pull out your phone and
light up the darkness to see that you are, indeed,
alone.

That took a strange turn indeed, I'll admit.
But isn't that just life? Even just a bit?
A series of twists and turns, subversions of
expectations,
Success and strife, every day and night,
innumerable frustrations.

But for now let's escape, for at least a little
while.
Life can be so intense, let us turn down the dial,
Take a moment to appreciate and on a different
perspective you'll draw,
Perhaps not a new lease on life but a renewed
sense of awe.

In appreciation of Cooking

Fizz, sizzle, crackle and pop!
Into the pan you go, plop plop plop.
"Hey, listen! And watch this cool trick I can
do!"
Great, there's now egg on the floor, but what
else is new?

It's a skill that needs timing, all your senses and
finesse,
Whether it's in your PJ's or whether you're
dressed to impress.
Poke it, waft it, take this teaspoon and try,
See the versatile potatoes mash, boil, bake and
fry.

Now fire up the oven and grab yourself a bowl,
Should I split this egg in half or just use it
whole?
One pinch, two pinch, three pinches, four,
You can't take it back but you can always add
more.

Once it's all combined, and layered just so,
You spread the final egg wash and it's ready to
go.
Until the timer beckons, you dare not open that
door.
But as you pace in anticipation, the aroma taunts
you even more.

Presentation is also important, though most
don't realise,
Cooking is more than just pleasing your
tastebuds, it's a feast for the eyes.
Regardless of your preference, whether savoury
or sweet,
Cooking is a delight and baking is such a treat.

In appreciation of Senses

Close your eyes and tell me this, what exactly do
you hear?
The serenity of silence, or an urban jungle
drawing near?
Actually pause for a moment now and practice
what I preach,
Observe the world around you, learn what it has
to teach.

Don't just look; touch, hear and smell,
And if you're game enough, taste as well.
Don't do it all at once, you must isolate your
focus,
Start from the very core of your being, your own
personal locus.

The epicentre of your thoughts will make this
hard to do,
But once you've done it once or twice, it will
come naturally to you.

Pick a sense to start with, touch may be a treat,
You will start to notice everything, from your
head right down to your feet.

The trickles of sensation across each and every
hair,
Is that a pain I feel? When did that get there?
Unsettled in your setting noticing everything
around,
Now redirect and then reflect on each and every
sound.

The humming of your fridge, the closing of a
door,
All these normal things around you'd never
noticed before,
Listen closely enough and you'll hear your
clothing rustle,
Tones typically tuned out by all the hustle and
bustle.

Scent is very much a gamble, for better or for
worse,
Treated by fragrant delights or smothered with a
dreadful curse,
Intoxicating, inebriating, does this smell off to
you?
Evolution's assistance in assessing danger in
something that's brand new.

Sight is a sense that I could, very easily, say so
much about,
It's the one we rely on most of the time until the
lights go out,
It works best of all when used in a team as looks
can be deceiving,
Critically assess and put to the test all the
information you are receiving.

Revenge is sweet, but dessert is sweeter, which
one will you choose?
Keep an open mind even if, sometimes, you just
might lose,
We do take for granted, at times, the senses that
we've got,
Not all folks are so fortunate as to have access to
the lot.

We drown our senses out at times, stepping back
from the world,
Blaring tunes or blinding lights, under a blanket
you have curled.
A fanfic or a TV Show, solace draws ever near,
Reflecting on what a marvel it is to exist on this
beautiful sphere.

In appreciation of Self Expression

When people find their calling, it's rarely clear right away,
Some forms of this may be average, experienced day to day.
While some may work hard at it, refining their chosen craft,
For others it comes far more naturally, their own personal raft.

All aboard and off we go, adventures so unknown,
Pull your oars out from the stream and who knows where you will flow.
A dancer, a prancer, a vibrato beau romancer,
A druid or elf paladin, a halfling necromancer.

From the land of facts and fallacies, the world is truly your oyster,
Out into the wilderness you go, released from your cloister.
Unsheltered and exposed, potential without a count,
Is this what a good life is? Yes! Without a doubt.

In appreciation of Family

How could I know,
   the ones I would not pick,
      Water runs well but our blood is
thick.
     We stick together wherever we are,
Sometimes it's near and often it's far.
    But as far back as I could recall,
      They are the ones to catch me,
  whenever I fall.

In appreciation of Traditions

Should you ask about tradition, a mixed
reception you will get,
For each soul will have their own, many of
which they'll never forget.
A culture that conditions, a doctrine of divine,
Which hand of cards will you be dealt based on
your bloodline?

You've heard the age-old adage, 'something old,
something new',
The bride scrambles frantically, "Can I borrow
something from you?!"
Of the last part she seems less panicked, maybe
it's not such a sin?
Unbeknownst to those around, the bluest lies
deep within.

One kiss upon each cheek is custom; some two,
some three or four,
For others you'll stay in your place, then bow
'til you see the floor.
A firm handshake, a hug or nod, which action
will you take?
If you do not know, then ask - it's better than
making a mistake.

It always seemed quite strange to follow ways
from days of old,
Not really knowing why, rather just doing what
one was told.
And though the concept may seem dated, many
things we've long outgrown,
There's nothing wrong with forming some new
traditions of our own.

In appreciation of Hope

A divisive concept to be sure,
Wishing and waiting for something more,
Something less, or something free,
Somewhere safe where you can just be.

For some it started as a dream on the eve of a
special day,
"And what do you wish for little one, little gent
and lady?"
A twinkle of wonder and a sprinkle of awe,
Contemplating the hope of something more.

Countless motives and drives alike,
Waiting for a win or inspiration to strike,
You should still work hard but for you I will
attest,
Let fate be your guide, close your eyes and hope
for the best.

In appreciation of Space

An infinite swirling chaos into the great beyond,
So recent are our discoveries there, so very very
young,
Unlike our endless universe in all its great
expanse,
Far greater than Australia, London, Rome or
France.

For as much progress as we've made,
There is much that's still unknown,
How impressive is our cosmos?
How much has it grown?

The beginning of time will give you clues,
Though small and so obscure,
Pondering too much will give you the blues.
But just enough to endure.

Galaxies and nebulae,
black holes, red dwarves and more,
Some seek to ascribe and to explain,
Others simply gaze along with awe.

Pretty colours and dazzling lights,
Some from planet Earth look no further,
Than the confines of their own back vines,
Not even our own planet do we nurture.

I prithee thee to take the time,
Go to the country, escape the confines,
Where light pollution cannot reach,
Go find the stars and count them each.

Alas. The stars that you see? They're mostly
dead,
But please don't let this fill you with dread,
They've lived their lives and so shall you,
Enjoy it while it's there, don't just make do.

We seek not to change, but to understand,
How the universe has been arranged and the
effects this has on man,
It all just seems too perfect, as if it were all
planned,
The middle part we know, but not the beginning,
nor the end.

Everything we've ever dreamed,
Every insight we've ever gleamed.
Occurred on this pale blue dot,
It isn't much, but it's quite a lot.

In appreciation of Critters

Round little fur ball,
I hear wheeking all around,
Chirping happy now.

Pink, long, skinny tail,
Twitchy nose and big round ears,
Hearing danger near.

Short, wet tail, now legs,
Quite a journey just to grow,
Hop, hop, off you go.

Long, dry, furry tail,
They can purr and they can wail,
Laser chase, ne'er fail.

Warm yet wet, cold home,
Don't take that rock! That is mine!
Against all odds, live.

Bark, pant, wag all day,
Melting all your fear away,
Man's best friend always.

Knock, tweet, sing and play,
Here's your favourite tune all day!
Bones light, heart is full.

Feet waddle slowly,
Orange bill and down to spare,
Anger in their eyes.

Home is my fortress,
Inside I am protected,
Snap! Nom! Lettuce leaf.

In appreciation of Perfectionism

Not wanting to begin for fear of the end,
A stranger isn't as kind as your family, nor
friends,
Scared of being creative, fearing taking the test,
Is the work you did just then really your very
best?

It's quality, not quantity that I have on my mind,
Alas, that notion is often discouraged in
conditions that are timed,
Even now I feel it so, the pressure that is due,
If we had free roam to call our own, how much
better would we do?

A series of questions and a catalogue of answers,
Mind wandering about like a chorus of dancers,
That knowledge I just had, where did it go?
It escaped down a path that I could not follow.

The time ticks onwards, driving me insane,
Thoughts that are expiring, rotting in my brain,
This isn't good enough, nor that, nor the rest,
Losing good ideas whilst searching for the best.

"What am I doing? This will never be good
enough",
As I drag my ideas through the muck and the
rough.
The harshest critic? Yes, that is I,
Unfavourably biased until the day that I die.

In appreciation of Science

The whispers in the breeze,
They bring me to my knees,
Among the gentle trees,
I find my peace.

The paperbark is peeling,
Nature slowly healing,
Bloodwood trees revealing,
The power from within.

It was the bubbles and the colour,
That bemused me like no other,
I'm telling Papa and Mama,
I think that I'm in love.

It was the converging of the plates,
That drew me near to fate,
I hope that I'm not late,
To discover so much more.

Round and round and round we go,
Where it will stop, nobody knows,
The field of mine will always grow,
Humbled forever where I am home.

Inspired as a child,
My love for it grew wild,
In no way was it mild,
I have found my call.

In appreciation of Love

Words, affection, a fluffy cuddly bear,
Fingers running through your freshly brushed
hair.
A heart, a rose, a note written in red,
A warm embrace, entirely interlaced, as you
retire to bed.
Love is a language that you'll learn all on your
own.
Love is often the reason you'll smile at a
perfume or cologne.
Speaking in tongues your entire life until
someone finally understands,
The reason your heart beats so much, when all
they did was hold your hands.

Love is ever-evolving. It changes, don't you
know?
That's why we say such things as, a love that
will only grow.
Love learns what you want and always what you
need,

Though love can turn dangerous when it is
fuelled by greed.
As much as it tries to convince you, false love is
such a sneak,
It tells you what you want to hear until your
resolve grows weak.
It's hard to tell the difference, but through
experience you'll get to know,
Someone who makes you smile, from the person
who makes you glow.

Your language stems from how you were loved
right at the very start,
Though you may not know it, right away, you'll
feel it within your heart.
Gifts, silk words, an "I love you", a touch that
never fades,
breakfast in bed while you rest your head or time
that's given in spades,
Love is respecting yourself enough to know
when to let go,
Knowing when to say yes and when to say no.
Love is a sacrifice, it's like sharing your soul
through song,
but if it means sacrificing who you are, then I'm
afraid you're doing it wrong.

Some say that love is an open door, but I tend to
disagree,
Love, to its most basic form, is vulnerability.
Elevated heart rate, an unmoving gaze,
A smile you can't get out of your mind, even
after several days.
A deer in headlights no less, rose coloured or
not,
A feeling, I imagine, akin to being shot.
Love is vulnerability, some will rise and some
will fall,
And yet the true vulnerability lies with those
who have never loved at all.

Love is bittersweet, no matter how hard you try.
To force it would be a fool's errand and soon
that love would die.
They say to succeed in love is to take it into your
own hands,
But even if that works for a little while, the
universe may have other plans.
I do believe in a reality where things would have
worked with you,
But time has gone by, my hands are tied. There's
nothing I can do.

In appreciation of Tears

Happy or sad, this reaction does not
discriminate,
Powerful emotions from you will emanate,
Often as a child, potentially less so once you've
grown,
As you graze your knee, or while in bed all
alone.

Evolution wise we see an empowered
adaptation,
Blocking out potential sources of infestation,
Pollen drifting on the wind, a message oh so
solemn,
May not be a solution but an ease to every
problem.

Water, salts and lysozymes, they're good for
your skin,
Had a rough day at the office? Let yourself cave
in.
Sacrifice some time, you'll feel better once it's
done,
Let them all break free and down your cheeks
they'll run.

In appreciation of Music

The power of music,
It soothes the soul.
From jazz and ballet,
To hard rock 'n' roll.

A deep touching tune,
Emotions out of control,
Who can really judge,
When you give it your heart-whole.

You might produce,
Mix, bellow and sing,
Make music your own,
It's a versatile thing.

It's what can unite us,
Make us tap, make us dance.
Make us feel deep emotions,
And get caught up in romance.

The power of music,
It heals the soul.
It can make you feel anything,
That is the goal.

In appreciation of Teachers

Holding a lot of influence for young
impressionable minds,
Get a good one from the start and you will break
free from your binds,
Challenging your beliefs, not out of spite but
self-reflection,
Doing their darndest to engage with various
vocal inflections.

Each teacher's quirks are their own, but all do
try to inspire,
To push you further than you know, reaching
forever higher,
A good teacher will drive you, the best will give
you the maps,
And let you explore all on your own, while
dodging all the traps.

Sometimes it might feel harsh, the feedback that they give,
But honesty is the best policy, not just in how we live,
You will not fight to be your best if you think you're already there,
We critique and praise you in good faith, all because we care.

In appreciation of Friends

Where would I be without my friends,
The first I turn to when trouble's around the
bend.
The ones I laugh with, those who love and care.
And those who will go out with me, regardless
of what I wear.

Friendships take effort, there's a give and take.
They can look out for you and it's all for your
sake.
They can be there for you in your times of need,
They seek your company for who you are, and
not out of greed.

You must offer back to friends, as much as you
can.
For they too depend on you, to lend a helping
hand.
When push comes to shove and it's all on the
line.
A true friend will always give you their time.

In appreciation of an Australian Summer

Wattle floats in a soft trickled creek,
The moonlit night, the summer heat.
Tossing and turning I hear the bats shriek,
I throw off the sheets and stand, sweat-drenched
feet.

I spring open a window, no comfort there.
I struggle down the hallway, topsy turvy,
I feel my back sweat cling to my hair,
I wonder if the headache will end, the world is
curvy.

A long night of fun, merriment and joy,
Followed by the somber trip down the hall.
A night out with mates, twas all a ploy,
To get me to stay up late again, I cling to the
wall.

I finish my business and head back to bed,
The summer fun lasts so long.
The long warm nights I await with dread,
And I seek comfort in those friendships,
lifelong.

In appreciation of Chance

Multiple realities, freedom of choice,
Being born into a country where I have a voice,
As a female, a leader, blazing my own path,
Not being the subject of someone else's wrath.

A lucky country they call us, that couldn't be
more true,
The freedom to take up hot pursuit for what I
want to do,
I am quite the fortunate one, I thank my lucky
stars.
That I have been born here and now, not once
we've left for mars.

What could have been, I wonder, if I were born
someone new,
Would I still be able to choose, would I still be
the lucky few?
To choose who I love, my future, my job and
passion,
To choose who I want to be, to have my own
sense of fashion?

Reality can be a fickle thing, who knows what's
coming your way,
Who knows what will the future bring, a chance
for you each day.
An opportunity to prove yourself, to be a better
you,
For each new time you make a choice, you
branch into someone new.

In appreciation of Daydreaming

Staring at a blank space,
There's nothing even there,
Yet it took me to a higher place,
Oh! The wonders I saw there.

What ifs, what could be and scenarios galore,
Even some ideas that I've never had before,
Actions made by a different person who
strangely resembled me,
Making choices that I myself never thought I
would be.

Staring at an open sky,
Water fluffy and white,
Watching myself on the silver screen,
Now that would be quite a sight.

Brought back to the playground, sunlight
warming up my skin,
Family all around, have I rubbed my sunscreen
all back in?

Sometimes the thoughts will stay, and others
they will go,
How the mind comes up with such things? I
doubt we'll ever know.

Staring into darkness,
Don't have to close your eyes,
Your thoughts here are your own,
There's no need to disguise.

It's not just bound by day,
It can also grace you at night,
At times they'll be the greatest things,
In others, they're such a fright.

In appreciation of Birthdays

Music and cake and merriment all 'round,
Your own special day no sadness should be
found,
Another trip 'round the sun you've made,
Another year filled with your escapades.

The early ones are only known by accounts told
second hand,
When you toddled around and only stood as tall
as auntie's hand,
Hey! You've reached double digits now and you
couldn't feel any wiser!
Spending on all the things you've wanted or
storing them like a miser.

Another year flies right on by, you're different
but much the same,
Maturing now and slightly jaded, life is no
longer just a game.
It's so much more, yet so much less, depending
on how you spend your time,
Enjoy the world and all it is, you're not limited
by your prime.

One more trip around the sun, but it's not the last
one yet,
Many memories you've made over time, hoping
not to forget,
Greying hair, and weathered skin, celebrating
your life so far,
They gather 'round and sing for you, to
remember who you are.

In appreciation of Farewell

One of the quirkiest things I've ever heard is that; Life is very akin to a toilet paper roll - the closer you get to the end, the faster it gets.
I won't tell you to live every moment as if it were your last because then you'll find yourself anticipating rather than enjoying life while you're in the moment. I do, however, as we reach the end of our journey implore you to be kind.

Life is fleeting and is far too short to forget to be kind.
Far too short to forget to smile when even an inkling of happiness crosses your mind.
Far too short to forget to express your gratitude, Accept early in life that those things are not just owed to you.
Far too short to forget to compliment one another,
For your words could be the ones that make a lasting impact, unlike any other.

And most certainly, life is far too short to try to deny yourself of who you are,
Deny yourself of that and you'll go merely a fraction as far.
As a wise author once said, "Those who mind don't matter and those who matter don't mind."
So go forth and be the best version of yourself, but most of all, be kind.